USING MATHS

EMERGENCY DEPARTMENT

by Hilary Koll, Steve Mills
and Dr Kerrie Whitwell

ticktock

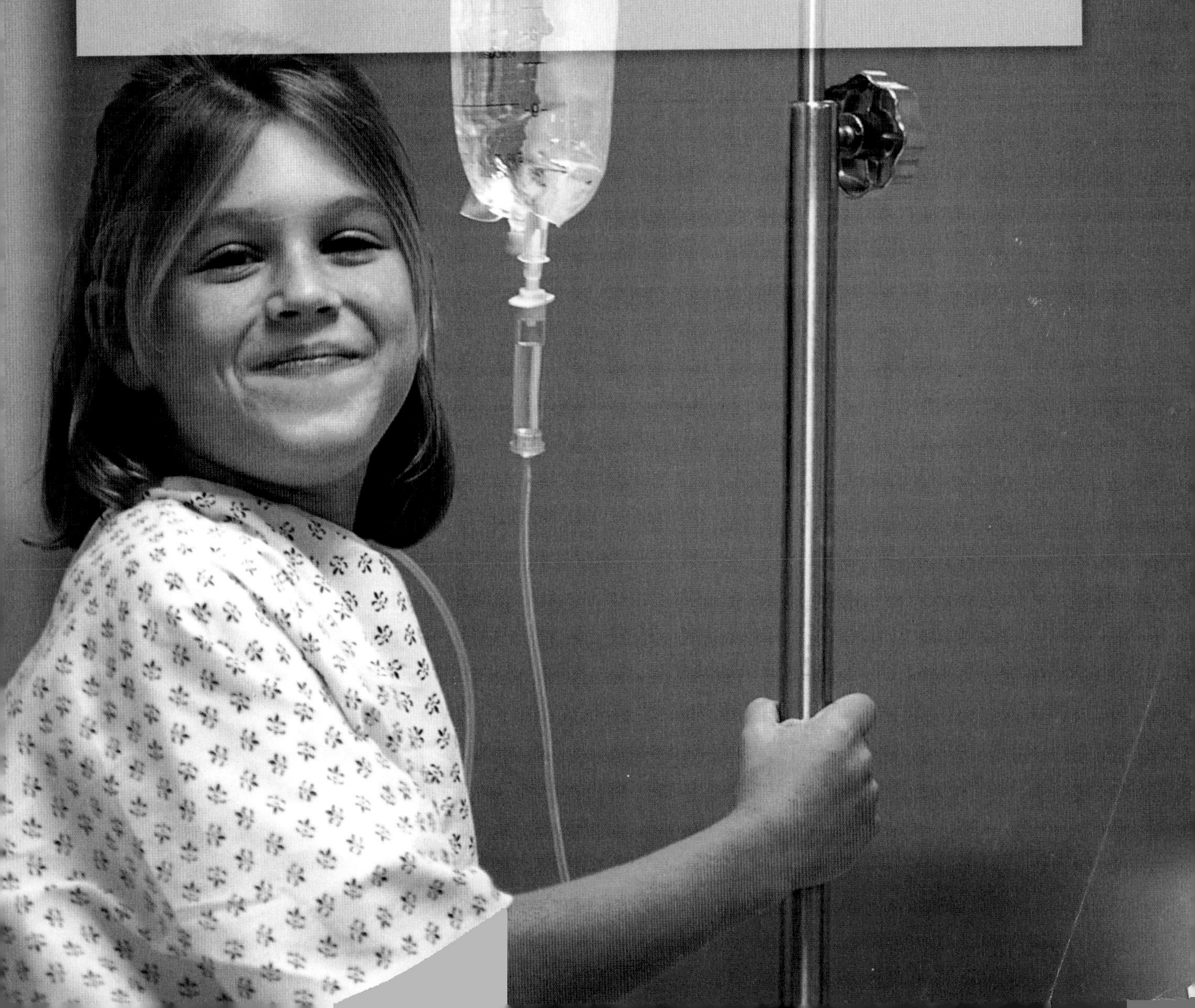

USING MATHS EMERGENCY DEPARTMENT

First published in Great Britain in 2006 by ticktock Media Ltd.,
Unit 2, Orchard Business Centre, North Farm Road, Tunbridge Wells, Kent, TN2 3XF

ISBN 1 86007 989 X
Printed in China

A CIP catalogue record for this book is available from the British Library.

HILARY KOLL

Hilary Koll (B.Ed. Hons) was a Leading Maths Teacher in a primary school before training as a Numeracy Consultant for the National Numeracy Strategy. She has worked as a Lecturer in Mathematics Education at the University of Reading, teaching on undergraduate, post-graduate and training courses. She is now a full-time writer and consultant in mathematics education. Hilary Koll and Steve Mills can be contacted via their website www.cmeprojects.com

STEVE MILLS

Steve Mills (B.A. Hons, P.G.C.E., M.Ed.) was a teacher of both primary and secondary age children and an LEA Maths Advisory Support Teacher before joining the University of Reading as a Lecturer in Mathematics Education. He worked with both under-graduate and post-graduate students in their preparation for teaching maths in schools. He has written many mathematics books for both teachers and children. Visit www.cmeprojects.com for details.

DR KERRIE WHITWELL

Dr Kerrie Whitwell (MBChB FRCS(Ed) FFAEM) has specialised in emergency medicine since 1998, and is a consultant at the Royal Free Hospital, at Hampstead in London. This busy emergency department sees over seventy thousand patients each year. In addition to the assessment and treatment of emergency patients, Dr Whitwell's work includes review clinics and the supervision of an observation ward. She has a particular interest in paediatric emergency medicine.

CONTENTS

NUMERACY WORK COVERED IN THIS BOOK:

CALCULATIONS:
Throughout this book there are opportunities to practise **addition, subtraction, multiplication** and **division** using both mental calculation strategies and pencil and paper methods.

NUMBERS AND THE NUMBER SYSTEM:
- COMPARING & ORDERING NUMBERS: pgs. 8, 9, 12, 13, 15, 16
- ESTIMATING: pg. 19
- FRACTIONS: pgs. 21, 23, 27
- NUMBER SEQUENCES: pg.18
- ROUNDING: pg. 11

SOLVING 'REAL LIFE' PROBLEMS:
- DATES: pgs. 8, 9
- DIRECTION: pg. 6
- DISTANCE: pg. 6
- MAPS: pg. 7
- MASS/WEIGHT: pgs. 20, 21
- TEMPERATURE: pgs. 14, 15
- TIME: pgs. 12, 1314, 24, 25

HANDLING DATA:
- PICTOGRAMS: pgs. 10, 11
- USING GRAPHS: pgs. 14, 15, 16, 17
- USING FORMULAS: pgs. 20, 21

MEASURES:
- RELATIONSHIPS BETWEEN UNITS OF MEASUREMENT: pg. 6

SHAPE AND SPACE:
- 2-D SHAPES: pgs. 22
- ANGLES: pg. 22
- LINE SYMMETRY: pg 22

Supports the maths work taught at Key Stage 2 and 3

HOW TO USE THIS BOOK

Maths is important in the lives of people everywhere. We use maths when we play a game, ride a bike, go shopping - in fact, all the time! Everyone needs to use maths at work. You may not realise it, but doctors and nurses would use maths during a busy day at an emergency department. With this book you will get the chance to try lots of exciting maths activities using real life data and facts about hospitals. Practise your maths and numeracy skills and experience the thrill of what it's really like to help patients get better.

This exciting maths book is very easy to use – check out what's inside!

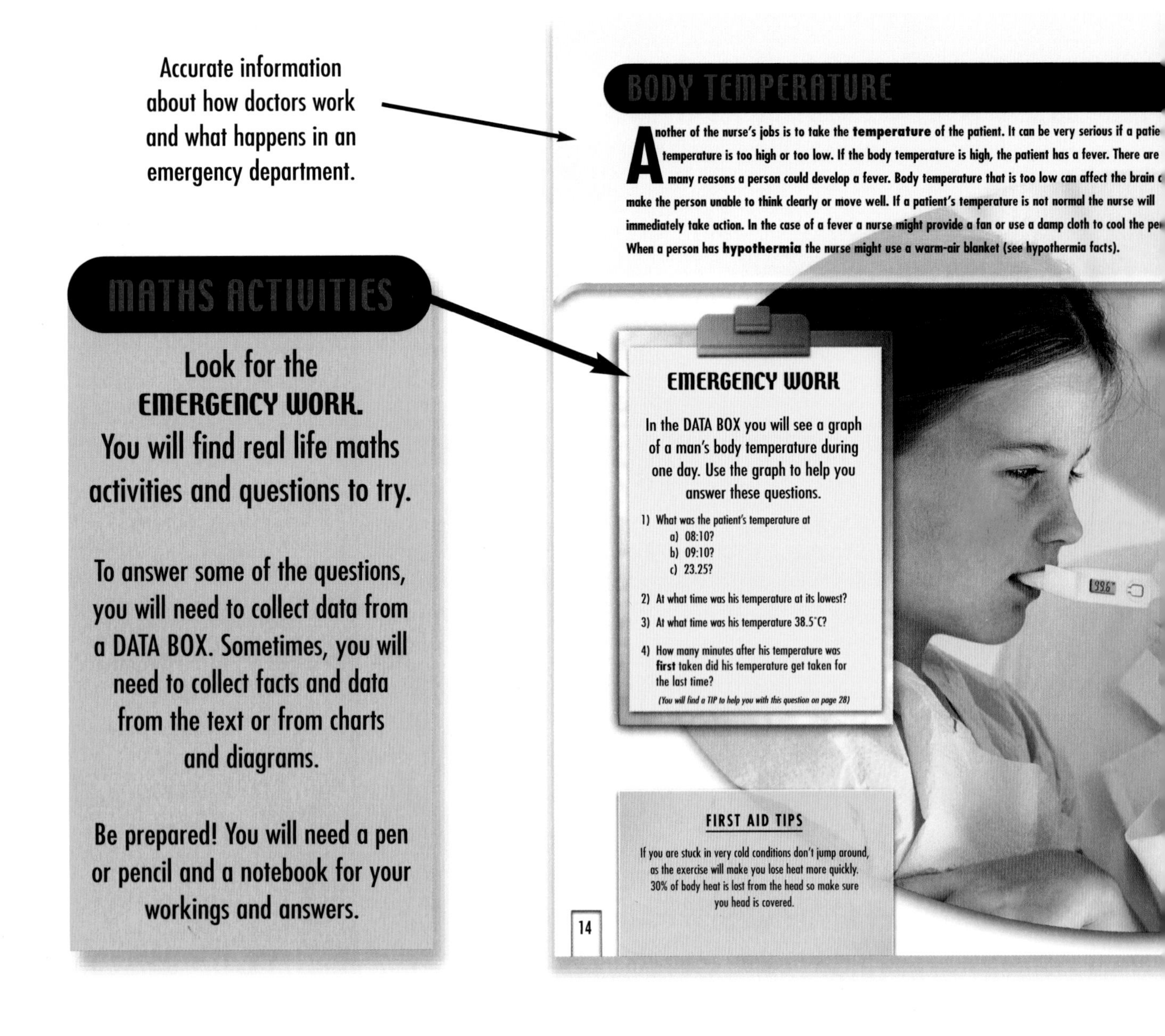

DATA BOX

If you see one of these boxes, there will be important data inside that will help you with the maths activities.

MATHS ACTIVITIES

Feeling confident? Try these extra **CHALLENGE QUESTIONS.**

EQUIPMENT FACTS

Many different types of electronic or digital thermometers are available. Some measure a person's temperature by putting the probe under the arm or in the mouth. Other thermometers measure a person's temperature by putting the probe in their ear; these are called tympanic thermometers. Mercury thermometers are rarely used nowadays because the mercury inside is dangerous. If a thermometer accidentally breaks it is very important to avoid getting the mercury on your skin.

DATA BOX TEMPERATURE CHART

Temperature is measured using a thermometer. The normal body temperature of humans is 37°C.

Fahrenheit °F: 93.2 95 96.8 98.6 100.4 102.2 104 105.8

Temperature Celsius °C: 34 35 36 37 38 39 40 41

If there is a problem, a nurse would take a patient's temperature many times over the course of a day to see whether it is rising or falling. This graph shows the temperature of a man during one day, after arriving in the emergency department at 8:00 a.m. The red dots show his temperature at various times. The red lines have been drawn to make the chart easier to read.

Time: 08.10 08.30 08.45 09.10 09.25 10.00 10.45 12.00 14.30 16.15 20.00 23.25

40°c 39°c 38°c 37°c 36°c

CHALLENGE QUESTION

Here are the average body temperatures of some animals.

Blue whale	35.5°C
Cow	38.5°C
Dog	38°C
Elephant	36.5°C
Ostrich	39°C
Owl	40°C
Polar bear	37°C

The DATA BOX above shows the average human temperature.

1) How much cooler or warmer are their bodies than the average human temperature?
2) Put the temperatures of these animals and birds in order, starting with the lowest temperature.

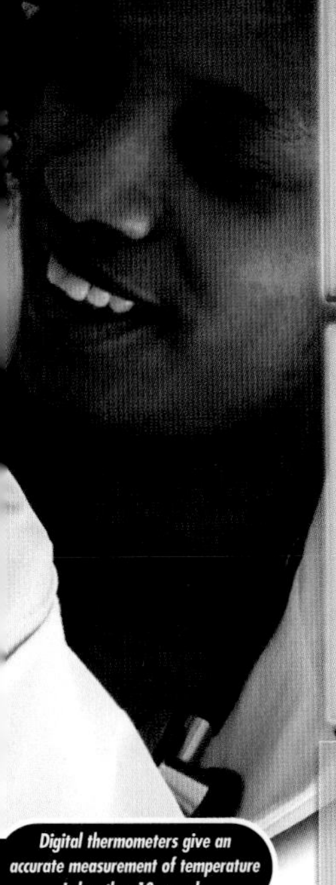

Digital thermometers give an accurate measurement of temperature in less than 10 seconds.

HYPOTHERMIA FACTS

Patients with dangerously low body temperatures are suffering from hypothermia. They are warmed up with a warm-air blanket. The blanket is made of two sheets of thin material filled with air. A special machine blows warm air into the blanket. It is placed on top of the patient like an extra warm duvet.

5

Fun to read facts and tips about what happens in the emergency department of a hospital

IF YOU NEED HELP...

TIPS FOR MATHS SUCCESS

On pages 28 – 29 you will find lots of tips to help you with your maths work.

ANSWERS

Turn to pages 30 – 31 to check your answers.
(Try all the activities and questions before you take a look at the answers.)

GLOSSARY

On page 32 there is a glossary of medical words and a glossary of maths words.
The glossary words appear **in bold** in the text.

THE EMERGENCY

Doctors and nurses in the emergency department of a hospital treat people with all kinds of problems. They have to know how to care for people who have been involved in an accident and for those who have become unwell very suddenly (such as those suffering from a **stroke** or an **asthma** attack). Some people make their own way to the hospital but in other cases an ambulance is called. The ambulance **paramedics** give first aid treatment and then take the patient to the local hospital, calling ahead to warn the hospital in advance if the problems are serious.

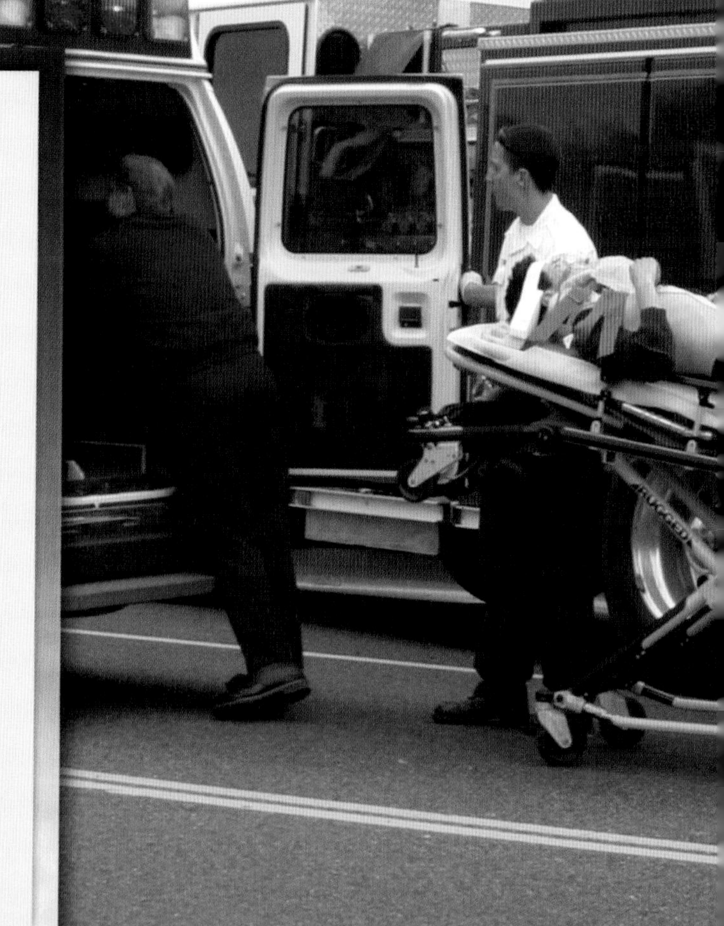

EMERGENCY WORK

Look at the map in the DATA BOX on page 7 and work out the shortest route to get from the hospital to the scene of the accident. The driver needs to know whether to turn **left** or **right** at each junction.

1) a) How many left turns do you make?
   b) How many right turns?

2) You choose a route to avoid traffic lights.
   a) How many left turns do you make?
   b) How many right turns?

3) As you drive your patient back to the hospital, you want to avoid the traffic light and the speed bumps.
   a) How many left turns do you make?
   b) How many right turns?

CHALLENGE QUESTIONS

Look at the map. Each square represents 100m.

1) What is the shortest distance from the scene of the accident to the hospital? How far is this in kilometres?
2) If 1.6 kilometres is about 1 mile, about how many miles is this distance?

(You will find a TIP to help you with these questions on page 28)

EMERGENCY DRIVING FACTS

Paramedics use flashing lights and a siren in an emergency. This is to alert people in the street to take extra care when crossing the road and to get the other vehicles to move out of the way.

Paramedics spend about three weeks learning how to drive an ambulance. At the end they have to take a test to check their advanced driving skills.

DATA BOX THE AMBULANCE'S ROUTE

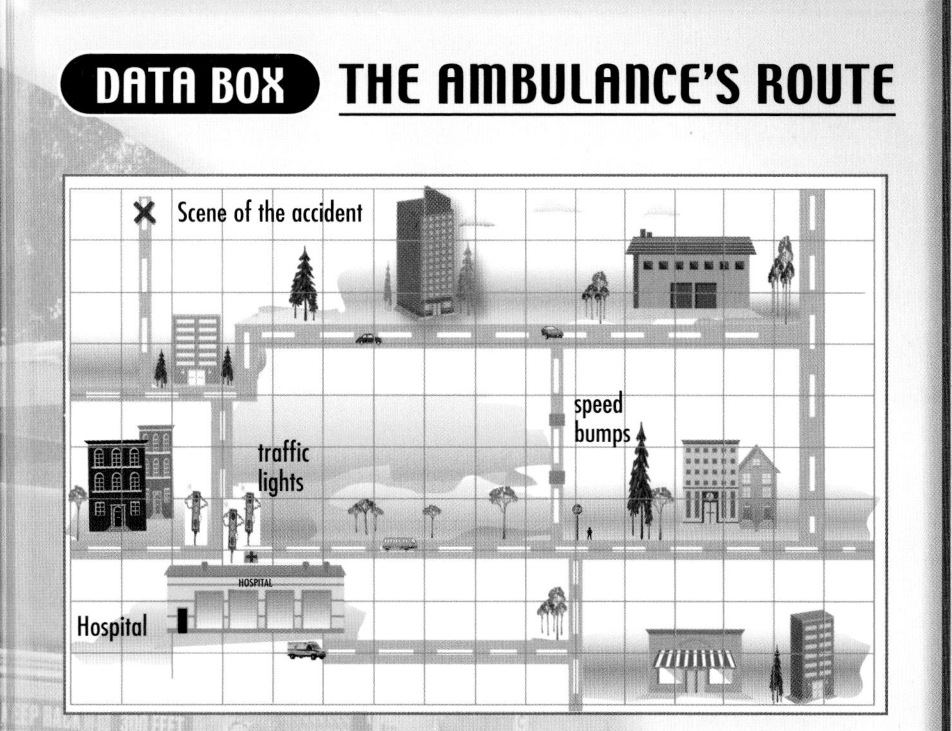

Scale of map:
—— = 100 metres

The paramedics who drive the ambulance must know the roads well and be clear on exactly where to go. Once they have carried out first aid, they must take the injured to the hospital as quickly as they can.

FIRST AID TREATMENTS

Paramedics carry out first aid treatments before they reach the hospital. Here are some of the ways they might help patients:

Arm injury	Put the arm in a sling.
Leg injury	Put a splint on the leg to stop it from moving.
Wound	Cover with a dressing.
Bleeding	Apply a dressing and a bandage. **Elevation** (raising in the air) also helps reduce the bleeding from the wound.
Pain	Give the patient a special gas to breathe which takes away the pain.
Unconscious	Lie patient on their side with the head tilted up slightly (the recovery position). This ensures they will not choke while unconscious.
Back/ neck injury	Strap patient to a special board with foam blocks either side of the head. This keeps the patient still and prevents any further injury to the neck or spine while the patient is being moved.

Paramedics use a stretcher called a gurney. The wheels mean it can be moved easily while keeping the patient still.

ARRIVING AT THE HOSPITAL

When a patient arrives at the emergency department, they are usually met by a **triage** (pronounced 'tree-ahj') nurse. The nurse finds out the patient's personal details. The hospital needs to know the patient's name, address, date of birth and medical history. The nurse also needs information about the patient's illness or injuries. The nurse must decide how serious the problems are and decide whether the patient needs urgent attention or not. In emergency departments, patients with the most serious problems are treated first and those with less serious problems must wait.

EMERGENCY WORK

DATA BOX 1 on page 9 shows six people's details taken by the triage nurse. Look at the dates of birth (DOB) and the other information.

1) How many months older than Claire Smith is Arthur Miller?
2) Can you work out the names of each person below? The speech bubbles might help you.

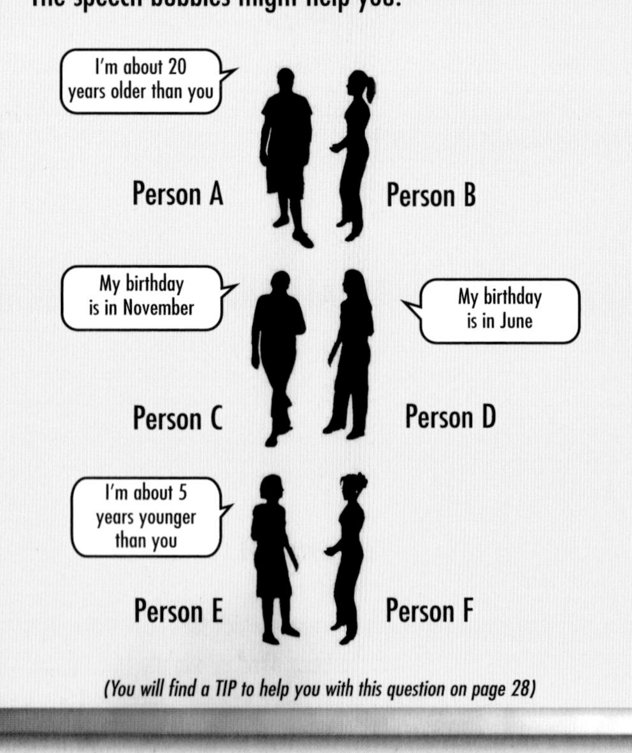

(You will find a TIP to help you with this question on page 28)

Patients who have difficulty breathing are put into the red triage category and are seen immediately.

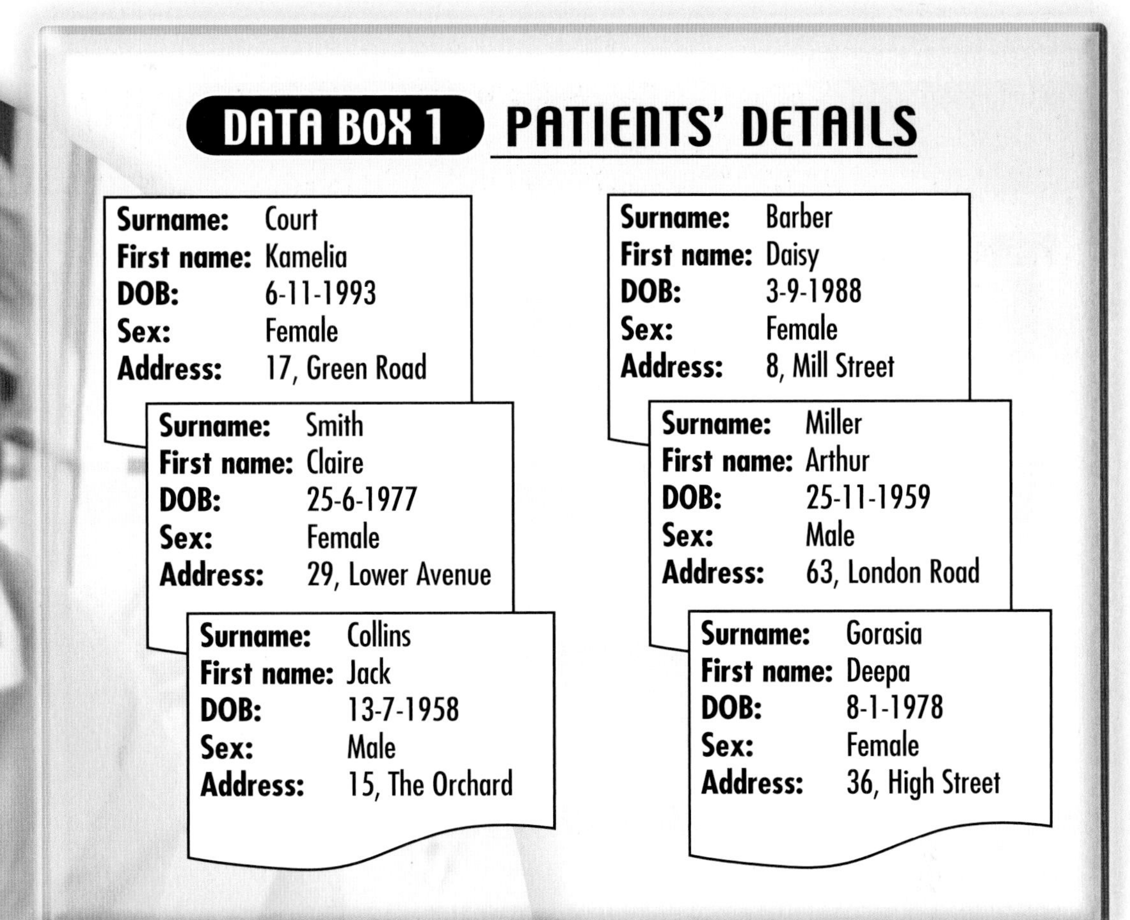

DATA BOX 1 PATIENTS' DETAILS

Surname: Court
First name: Kamelia
DOB: 6-11-1993
Sex: Female
Address: 17, Green Road

Surname: Smith
First name: Claire
DOB: 25-6-1977
Sex: Female
Address: 29, Lower Avenue

Surname: Collins
First name: Jack
DOB: 13-7-1958
Sex: Male
Address: 15, The Orchard

Surname: Barber
First name: Daisy
DOB: 3-9-1988
Sex: Female
Address: 8, Mill Street

Surname: Miller
First name: Arthur
DOB: 25-11-1959
Sex: Male
Address: 63, London Road

Surname: Gorasia
First name: Deepa
DOB: 8-1-1978
Sex: Female
Address: 36, High Street

DATA BOX 2

TRIAGE FACTS

The triage nurse puts the patients into a category according to their symptoms and assessment. This is printed on their information card to tell the doctor how unwell the patient is and how quickly they should be seen.

Triage Categories

Red – Immediate
Patient needs to be seen immediately

Orange – Very Urgent
Patient needs to be seen within ten minutes of arrival

Yellow – Urgent
Patient needs to be seen within one hour of arrival

Green – Standard
Patient should be seen within two hours of arrival

Blue – Non-Urgent
Patient should be seen within four hours of arrival

CHALLENGE QUESTION

Use the information in the two DATA BOXES on this page and these clues to work out which triage colour each of the six patients has been given. Write each patient's full name and triage colour.

- The youngest patient has difficulty breathing and needs to be seen immediately.
- The oldest patient has a sprained ankle should be seen within 2 hours of arrival.
- Daisy Barber has been given the 'Non-urgent' category.
- Claire Smith is bleeding and needs to be seen within ten minutes of her arrival.
- One other woman has burnt herself and needs to be seen within one hour of her arrival.
- The sixth patient has been put into the yellow category.

NURSING ASSESSMENT

The emergency department has several different areas and rooms. Each area has the specialist equipment that doctors might need. For example, the **resuscitation** room has equipment to help doctors restart a patient's heart. Children are taken to the **paediatric** area, which usually has toys to play with. Some patients are taken to a cubicle and others are asked to stay in the waiting area. A nurse assesses each patient and does a set of tests to check the patient's breathing, heart rate, blood pressure and **temperature** (we call these **vital signs**). The nurse will start to find out what the patient's problem might be.

EMERGENCY WORK

The DATA BOX on page 11 shows the most common reasons why people visit an emergency department. Look at the **pictogram** to see the problems and injuries that people had during one morning and how many people suffered from each condition.

Use the information in the pictogram to answer these questions.

1) What was the most common condition?
2) What was the least common condition?
3) How many patients were suffering from:
   a) chest pain?
   b) wounds?
   c) suspected broken bones?
   d) abdominal pain?
4) How many more patients had breathing difficulties than had chest pain?
5) How many fewer patients had wounds than had suspected broken bones?
6) How many patients were there in total?

(You will find a TIP to help you with this question on page 28)

*A **stethoscope** allows a doctor to listen to a patient's heart and lungs.*

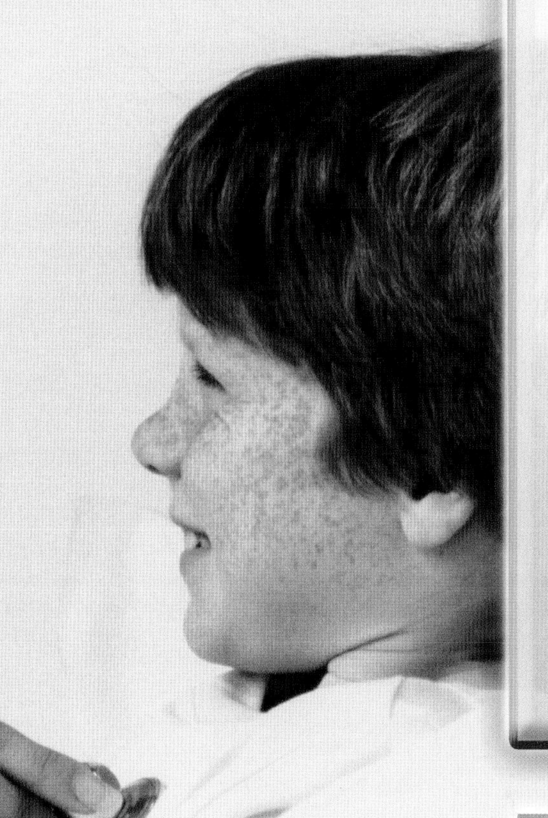

EMERGENCY FACTS

The triage nurse may carry out some tests to find out about a patient's condition.

- The nurse may place a probe on the patient's finger to measure the **pulse** electronically and check the oxygen levels in the blood.
- He or she may check the **respiratory** (breathing) rate if a patient has difficulty in breathing. The number of breaths in one minute is counted.
- The patient may also have his or her temperature taken.
- The triage nurse may also ask the patient for a specimen of urine or perform a skin prick test to find out about the patient's blood sugar level, particularly if they are diabetic.

DATA BOX

PATIENTS' CONDITIONS

A pictogram of the different conditions of patients attending the emergency department of a hospital in one morning

Key ☹ = 4 people

Wounds	☹☹☹☹
Suspected broken bones	☹☹☹☹☹☹◐
Unconscious or semiconscious	☹◐
Chest pain	☹☹☹
Difficulty breathing	☹☹☹◐
Abdominal pain	☹☹◐
Other	☹☹☹☹

CHALLENGE QUESTION

If an emergency department treats about 250 patients a day, about how many patients will be treated each year? Give your answer to the nearest 10,000 people.

HEART RATE AND BLOOD PRESSURE

Measuring someone's pulse means finding out how quickly their heart is beating and whether it is beating regularly, at its normal rhythm. There are many reasons a patient's **pulse rate** might be high, such as having done exercise, being in shock, or having heart difficulties. The heart rate can also be listened to using a **stethoscope.** At the same time as measuring the heart rate, a nurse at the emergency department will also measure blood pressure. This is to find out how hard the blood is being pushed around the body. In serious cases a person might be attached to a heart rate monitor, which is a machine that shows the heart beat on a screen.

EMERGENCY WORK

In the DATA BOX on page 13 you will see a table showing the expected pulse rates of children and adults of different ages. A nurse must decide if a child or adult has a pulse rate outside the range shown, which might tell them that there is a problem.

The information below shows the number of times 6 children's hearts beat in 15 seconds. Work out each person's pulse rate per minute. Use the information in the DATA BOX table to decide which of these children have a problem with their pulse rate.

Name	Age	Number of times heart beats in 15 seconds
Jane	4 years	25
Luke	6 months	35
Dev	7 years	36
Urvi	13 years	29
Molly	1 year	31
Chelsea	9 years	19

(You will find a TIP to help you with this question on page 28)

A sphygmomanometer measures blood pressure.

DATA BOX

PULSE RATE

A person's pulse rate is the number of heart beats per minute. The resting pulse rate is how fast it beats when the person is not doing any exercise. This table shows the expected pulse rates of children of different ages.

Age Range	*Number of beats per minute*
under 12 months	between 110 and 160
1-2 years	between 100 and 150
3-5 years	between 95 and 140
6-12 years	between 80 and 120
over 12 years	between 60 and 100

To measure heart rate the number of times the heart beats in 15 seconds (one quarter of a minute) is counted and then this number is multiplied by 4. This tells you the number of beats per minute.

CHALLENGE QUESTION

The pulse rates of 6 adults are shown here. How many times would each person's heart beat in 15 seconds (one quarter of a minute)?

a) 92 beats per minute
b) 76 beats per minute
c) 52 beats per minute
d) 72 beats per minute
e) 68 beats per minute
f) 88 beats per minute

(You will find a TIP to help you with this question on page 28)

HEART FACTS

Some patients who are awaiting their test results are put on a heart rate monitor. This displays the heart rate on a screen so that everyone knows immediately if there is a problem. Patients may be put on a monitor if their heart rate is very slow (less than 60 beats per minute), very fast (more than 120 beats per minute) or if the heart beat is irregular. Very sick patients and patients who have pains in their chest also have their heart rate monitored.

BLOOD PRESSURE FACTS

Blood pressure is measured using a sphygmomanometer (pronounced spig-mo-man-o-meter). An inflatable cuff is placed around the top of the patient's arm. The nurse puts a stethoscope on the arm in front of the elbow and blows up the cuff so that it is tight around the arm. As the air is let out of the cuff the sound of the heart beating can be heard through the stethoscope. The nurse takes readings from the pressure gauge.

BODY TEMPERATURE

Another of the nurse's jobs is to take the **temperature** of the patient. It can be very serious if a patient's temperature is too high or too low. If the body temperature is high, the patient has a fever. There are many reasons a person could develop a fever. Body temperature that is too low can affect the brain and make the person unable to think clearly or move well. If a patient's temperature is not normal the nurse will immediately take action. In the case of a fever a nurse might provide a fan or use a damp cloth to cool the person. When a person has **hypothermia** the nurse might use a warm-air blanket (see hypothermia facts).

EMERGENCY WORK

In the DATA BOX you will see a graph of a man's body temperature during one day. Use the graph to help you answer these questions.

1) What was the patient's temperature at
   a) 08:10?
   b) 09:10?
   c) 23.25?
2) At what time was his temperature at its lowest?
3) At what time was his temperature 38.5°C?
4) How many minutes after his temperature was **first** taken did his temperature get taken for the last time?

(You will find a TIP to help you with this question on page 28)

FIRST AID TIPS

If you are stuck in very cold conditions don't jump around, as the exercise will make you lose heat more quickly. 30% of body heat is lost from the head so make sure you head is covered.

EQUIPMENT FACTS

Many different types of electronic or digital thermometers are available. Some measure a person's temperature by putting the probe under the arm or in the mouth. Other thermometers measure a person's temperature by putting the probe in their ear; these are called tympanic thermometers. Mercury thermometers are rarely used nowadays because the mercury inside is dangerous. If a thermometer accidentally breaks it is very important to avoid getting the mercury on your skin.

DATA BOX TEMPERATURE CHART

Temperature is measured using a thermometer. The normal body temperature of humans is 37°C.

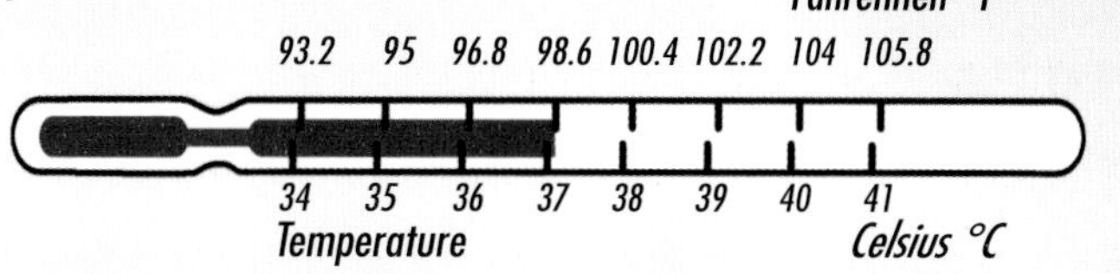

If there is a problem, a nurse would take a patient's temperature many times over the course of a day to see whether it is rising or falling. This graph shows the temperature of a man during one day, after arriving in the emergency department at 8:00 a.m. The red dots show his temperature at various times. The red lines have been drawn to make the chart easier to read.

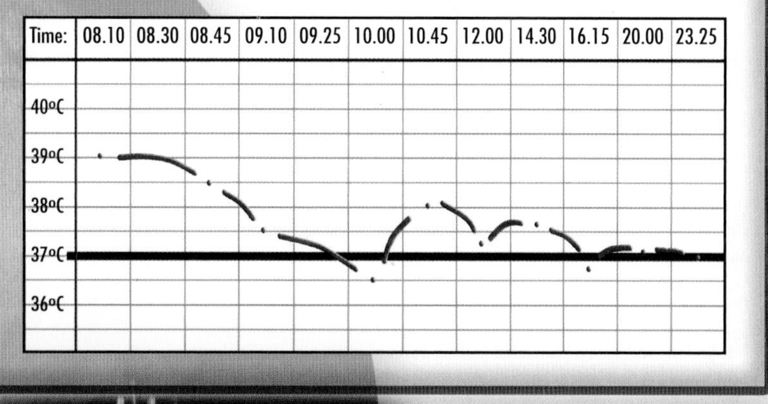

CHALLENGE QUESTION

Here are the average body temperatures of some animals.

Blue whale	35.5°C
Cow	38.5°C
Dog	38°C
Elephant	36.5°C
Ostrich	39°C
Owl	40°C
Polar bear	37°C

The DATA BOX above shows the average human temperature.

1) How much cooler or warmer are their bodies than the average human temperature?
2) Put the temperatures of these animals and birds in order, starting with the lowest temperature.

HYPOTHERMIA FACTS

Patients with dangerously low body temperatures are suffering from hypothermia. They are warmed up with a warm-air blanket. The blanket is made of two sheets of thin material filled with air. A special machine blows warm air into the blanket. It is placed on top of the patient like an extra warm duvet.

Digital thermometers give an accurate measurement of temperature in less than 10 seconds.

BREATHING

An emergency department often treats people with breathing difficulties such as **asthma** attacks. Asthma is the most common cause of breathing difficulty in children. Asthma is an illness where the air passages you breathe through tighten. This causes wheezing and makes breathing difficult. When an asthmatic patient arrives in the hospital a nurse will usually ask them to blow into a **peak flow meter**. This piece of equipment measures how much breath is blown out in under a second. This will tell the nurse how serious the patient's condition is and help him or her to decide on the treatment.

EMERGENCY WORK

In DATA BOX 1 on page 17 you will see some measurements in a table.

What is the **difference** between the expected and actual readings of:

a) Ella
b) Robbie
c) Ben
d) Zack
e) Jess

CHALLENGE QUESTIONS

Use the graph in DATA BOX 2 on page 17 to help you answer these questions.

1) Find the approximate expected peak flow rates for each of these heights:
   a) 138 cm
   b) 156 cm
   c) 114 cm

2) Find the approximate expected heights for each of these peak flow rates:
   a) 210 **l/min**
   b) 370 l/min
   c) 500 l/min

(You will find a TIP to help you with these questions on page 29)

A patient with asthma blows out into a peak flow meter.

DATA BOX 1 PEAK FLOW METER

The amount of breath children can blow out is usually related to how tall they are. Taller children generally blow out more than smaller children.

People who have asthma aren't able to blow out as much and show lower readings on the peak flow meter. For example:

Ella, an 8 year old girl, is 130cm tall. Normally, the peak flow reading of someone her age and height would be 260 l/min but Ella suffers from asthma and it is only 150 l/min. This is shown in the first row of the table.

Peak flow readings		
Name	**Expected reading (l/min)**	**Actual reading (l/min)**
Ella	260	150
Robbie	470	300
Ben	330	190
Zack	210	170
Jess	520	380

DATA BOX 2 PEAK FLOW AT VARIOUS HEIGHTS

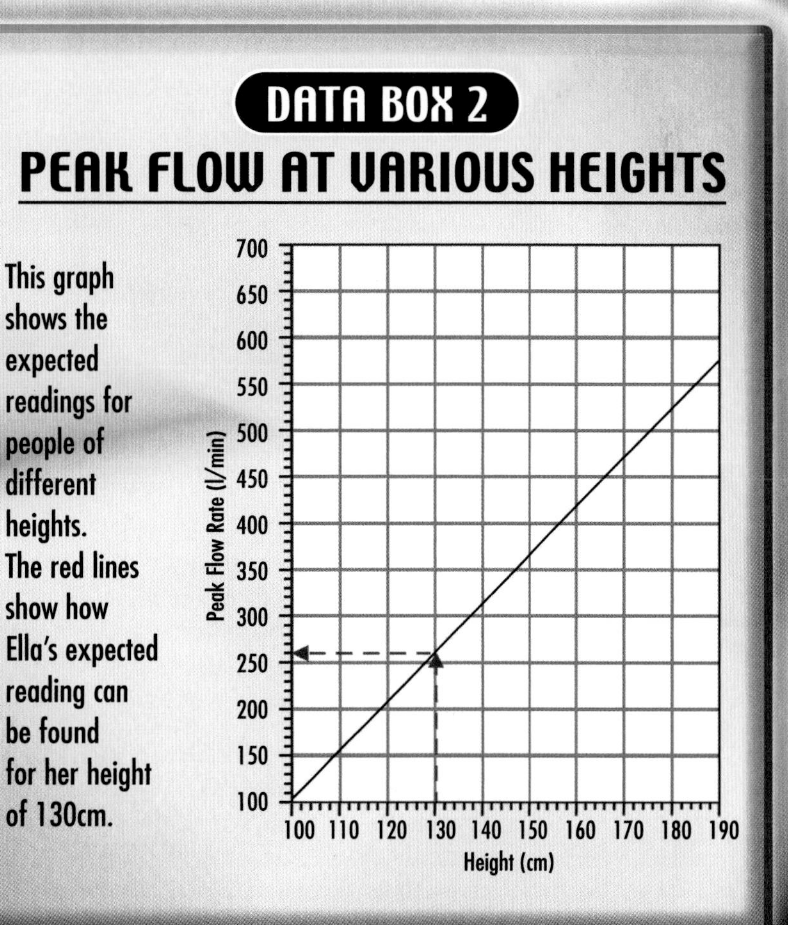

This graph shows the expected readings for people of different heights. The red lines show how Ella's expected reading can be found for her height of 130cm.

FURTHER TESTING

When the initial assessments have been made about the patient's condition, it might still not be clear what the problem is. Further testing can be carried out either by checking the blood and the urine for diseases or by using scanning equipment. Scans are performed using equipment such as ultrasound, CT or MRI machines. These further tests, which are called **'investigations'**, can help the doctors to decide what might be causing the problems and how best to treat them. Some patients will be given further tests immediately. Others will be sent home and asked to come back for the tests at a later date.

EMERGENCY WORK

When monitoring and checking people's heart, blood or **pulse rate** you need to be good at recognising whether the numbers are increasing or decreasing in value, and by how much. You also need to be good at predicting what might happen next.

Practise this by working out the next 3 numbers in each of these **sequences**.

a) 2, 4, 6, 8, 10, 12, ...
b) 100, 90, 80, 70, 60, 50, 40 ....
c) 25, 30, 35, 40, 45, 50, 55, 60 ....
d) 3, 6, 9, 12, 15, 18, ...
e) 2, 7, 12, 17, 22, 27, 32, 37...
f) $2\frac{1}{4}$, $2\frac{3}{4}$, $3\frac{1}{4}$, $3\frac{3}{4}$, $4\frac{1}{4}$, $4\frac{3}{4}$, $5\frac{1}{4}$, ...
g) -7, -4, -1, 2, 5, 8 ...
h) 1.5, 3, 4.5, 6, 7.5, ...
i) 0.9, 1.1, 1.3, 1.5, 1.7, ...

(You will find a TIP to help you with this question on page 29)

Doctors discuss what further tests a patient will need.

BLOOD FACTS

In an adult, the blood volume is approximately 7% of body weight.
A 100kg man has approximately 7 litres of blood.
A 70kg man has approximately 5 litres of blood.
A 50kg man has approximately $3\frac{1}{2}$ litres of blood.

For a child the amount of blood is found (in millilitres) by multiplying the child's weight in kilograms by 80.
A 10kg child has approximately 800 millilitres of blood.
Children have less blood compared with adults, so special small blood bottles are used for babies and small children.
All of these bottles hold 1ml of blood.

DATA BOX

BLOOD BOTTLES OF DIFFERENT SIZES

When blood is taken to be tested it is put into a 'blood bottle'. Blood bottles come in different sizes and each size has a different coloured top.

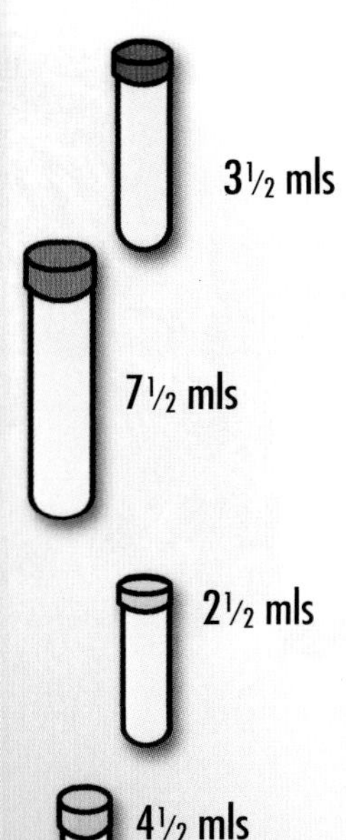

Red top bottles hold 3 ½ mls (millilitres) of blood. They are used for checks to see whether a patient is anaemic (has too few red blood cells).

Brown top bottles hold 7 ½ mls. They are used when checking the body salts of a patient.

Yellow top bottles hold 2½ mls. These are used when checking sugar levels.

Blue top bottles hold 4 ½ mls of blood. These are used to find out which type of blood a person has. There are four different blood groups, A, B, O and AB. Most people are either blood group O or A.

CHALLENGE QUESTION

A nurse uses three of the blood bottles shown in the DATA BOX on this page. He fills them all with blood.

What colour are the tops of the 3 bottles if together they hold a total of:

a) 10.5ml
b) 13.5ml
c) 14.5ml
d) 15.5ml

TREATMENTS

When the initial assessments have been made about the patient's injuries and condition, a doctor will decide on the treatment necessary. Treatments include putting a broken limb in plaster, **prescribing** a course of tablets, giving a patient an injection or even an operation. The doctor will explain to the patient what is happening and why. When deciding how much of a drug to use, a nurse or doctor sometimes needs to think about how old the patient is or how much they weigh. If they give an injection, children would need much less of the drug than an adult would.

EMERGENCY WORK

In the DATA BOX on page 21 you will see the names of some different injections and the amount per kilogram needed for children.

1) Work out how much antibiotic injection to give a child that is:
a) 17 kilograms b) 24 kilograms c) 16 kilograms

2). Work out how much painkiller injection to give a child that is:
a) 15 kilograms b) 13 kilograms c) 19 kilograms

3) Work out how much **steroid** injection to give a child that is:
a) 25 kilograms b) 30 kilograms

4) Work out how much **antihistamine** injection to give a child that is:
a) 20 kilograms b) 35 kilograms

(You will find a TIP to help you with these questions on page 29)

MEDICINE FACTS

Medicine that is taken by mouth (orally) can either be a tablet, capsule or a liquid. Tablets and capsules are fixed doses of medicine. Children are normally given liquid medicine so that smaller doses can be given. Also, it is easier to swallow than tablets or capsules.

Patients who suffer with difficulty in breathing, for example **asthma**, may be given medicine that is breathed in from their mouth straight into the lungs. These patients are given an '**inhaler**'.

DATA BOX

HOW MUCH MEDICINE TO GIVE TO A CHILD

The amount of medicine needed for a child is much less than that for an adult. When deciding how much medicine to give to a child, the doctor or nurse needs to know how old the patient is or how much they weigh.

Here is a list of how different doses might be calculated for children, to find how many **millilitres** of injection to give.

Antibiotic — **Weigh the child to find his or her mass (in kilograms).** The answer tells you how many millilitres (ml) of antibiotic injection to use if the number is 20 or less. If the number is greater than 20 give 20ml only.

Painkillers — **Divide the child's mass (in kilograms) by 10**. The answer tells you how many millilitres (ml) of painkilling injection to use.

Steroid — **Multiply the child's mass (in kilograms) by 4 and then divide by 100**. This is how many millilitres (ml) of steroid injection to use.

Antihistamine — **Double the child's mass (in kilograms) and then divide by 100.** This is how many millilitres (ml) of antihistamine injection to use.

A doctor cleans a patient's arm with an antiseptic wipe before giving an injection.

CHALLENGE QUESTION

Some of these cards show **fractions** and others show divisions.
Match pairs of cards that would give the same answer:

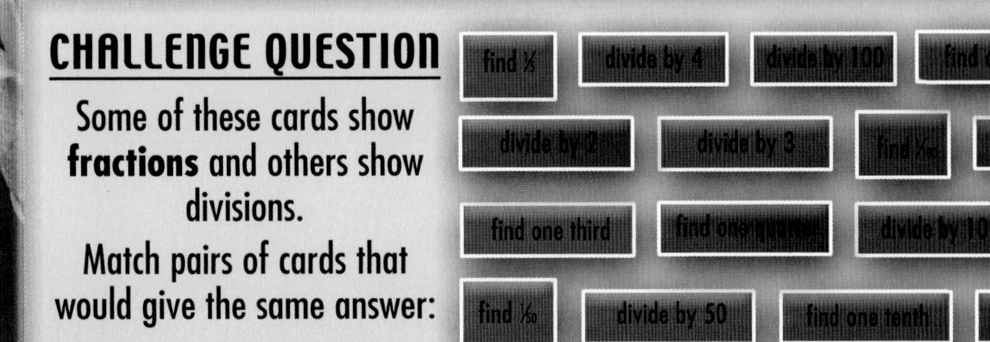

BROKEN BONES

Some of the most common injuries treated in accident and emergency are sprains and broken bones. To find out if someone has broken a bone, an x-ray is taken. The person that takes the x-ray is called a **radiographer.** The patient is taken into a special room and has an x-ray machine positioned above the injured part. The radiographer estimates the dose of radiation and the exposure time needed to get a good picture. This is entered into a computer which does the rest. At a press of a button the x-ray is taken and the film is processed in a big machine similar to that which develops normal photographs. The film is then ready for the doctor to look at.

EMERGENCY WORK

A sling is normally made from a triangular piece of material.

1) Identify each sling as a **scalene**, **isosceles** or **equilateral** triangle.

a b c

d e f

2) Which of these triangles have a right-angle?
3) Write the number of lines of reflective symmetry of each of these triangles.

(You will find a TIP to help you with these questions on page 29)

TREATMENT FACTS

Bones are held together by **ligaments** and a sprain occurs when a ligament has been stretched. If somebody has sprained his or her ankle it needs to be rested and elevated (lifted up). Ice can help to reduce the swelling. Sometimes, a support bandage may be put on the ankle. These bandages are tubes of elasticated material. A sprained wrist also needs to be rested and may be put into an arm sling. Slings are made from triangular pieces of material.

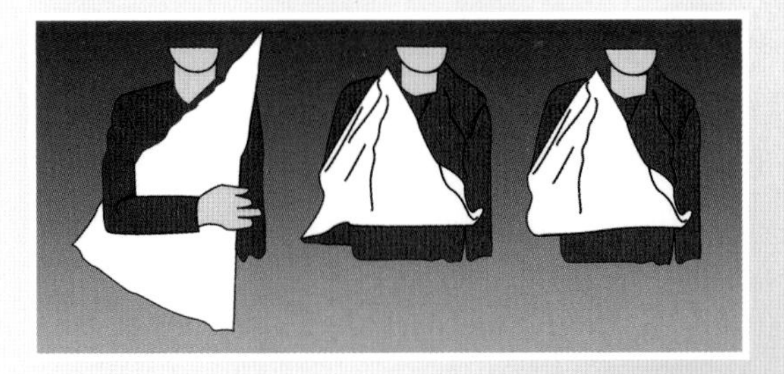

You could make a sling out of a square scarf folded in half diagonally.

DATA BOX

DIFFERENT X-RAY DOSES

Part of Body	Dose
Arm	4
Leg	5
Knee	3
Elbow	3
Ankle	2
Wrist	1
Hip	40
Chest	2
Skull	50
Abdomen	70

An x-ray machine uses doses of radiation when taking a picture of parts of the body. Too much radiation can be dangerous. The people working the machines (radiographers) must wear special badges to show how much radiation they are exposed to when they are working. Different doses of radiation are needed for x-raying different parts of the body. The dose depends on the size of the patient and the area that is being x-rayed. The table shows the different doses for each body part in a child.

Doctors look at an x-ray picture to see whether a bone has been broken.

CHALLENGE QUESTIONS

Look at the DATA BOX above. Each x-ray dose is equivalent to 1½ days of background radiation, so the x-ray for an ankle is equivalent to 3 days of background radiation.

How many days of background radiation is equivalent to an x-ray on the:

a) arm?
b) elbow?
c) wrist?
d) leg?
e) hip?
f) skull?
g) abdomen?

DRUG CHART

While the patients are still in the emergency department the doctor needs to write her summary. This records what treatments have been given to the patient and suggests what should happen next. Some patients might be **discharged** (allowed home) whilst others might be transferred to other wards in the hospital. Before a doctor **prescribes** a drug he or she checks that the patient is not already taking anything that may react with the drug that she is giving. The doctor also makes sure that the patient does not have any allergies. The doctor then needs to write a 'drug chart' for each patient.

EMERGENCY WORK

In the DATA BOX on page 25 you will see a table showing the number of tablets required per day and how many days the patient should take these.

1) Use the information to find how many tablets will be taken in total by :
   a) Ivor Pain
   b) Justin Bed
   c) Ivan Itch
   d) Seymour Days

2) The doctor said that each patient had to take two of their tablets at a time, at regular intervals during the day (24 hours). How many hours apart would the tablets be taken by:
   a) Ivor Pain
   b) Justin Bed
   c) Ivan Itch
   d) Seymour Days

A regular interval means that a period of time is split into equal parts.

A patient's records will help doctors decide how much medicine to give.

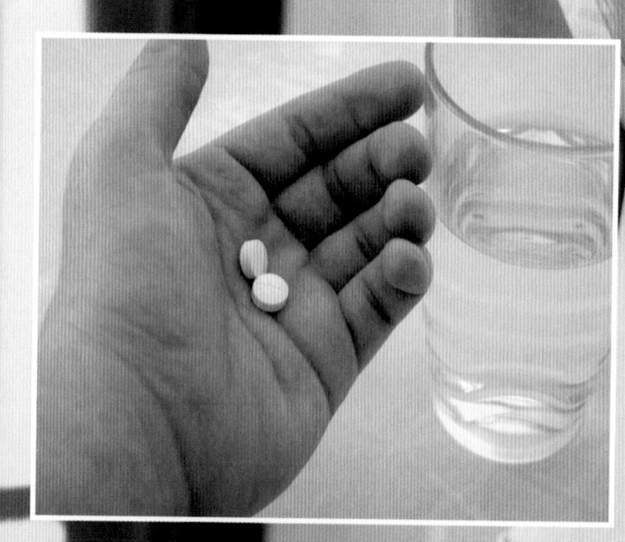

Most medicine for adults is given in the form of tablets.

DATA BOX MEDICINE CYCLES

Name of patient	Drug	Number of tablets per day	Number of days
Ivor Pain	Steroid tablets	8	3
Justin Bed	Antihistamines	6	2
Ivan Itch	Antibiotics	4	5
Seymour Days	Painkillers	8	7

Some medicines are given at regular time intervals throughout the day and some medicines, like painkillers are given when a patient needs them. A doctor may give specific instructions, such as one or two tablets should be taken every six hours if needed.

CHALLENGE QUESTION

Give your answers in twenty-four hour time

1) A patient is to take a tablet every 6 hours for 24 hours.
   a) If the first tablet was taken at 08.00 what times are the other tablets taken?
   b) If the first tablet was taken at 16.15 what times are the other tablets taken?

2) A patient is to take a tablet every 4 hours for 24 hours.
   a) If the first tablet was taken at 19:00 what times are the other tablets taken?
   b) If the first tablet was taken at 04:45 what times are the other tablets taken?

(You will find a TIP to help you with these questions on page 29)

MEDICINE FACTS

Medicines have two names. One is the 'generic' name, which is the ingredient of the tablet or injection. The other name is the 'trade' name, which is the name given to the medicine by the company that makes it. For example, paracetamol is the generic name for a type of pain killer. Trade names for paracetamol include Panadol and Tylenol.

WHAT HAPPENS NEXT?

The role of the emergency department is to provide care for cases that need immediate treatment. Once the emergency has been dealt with, the patient is moved out of the department. If the injury is not too serious, the patient is sent home (**discharged**). Other patients are moved to another ward in the hospital for further treatment. Some patients are admitted to a ward for **observation,** particularly if they have had a head injury or extremely high **temperature.** The emergency doctor might ask for a patient to be looked at frequently and have their **vital signs** checked regularly to monitor their condition.

EMERGENCY WORK

In the DATA BOX on page 27 you will see a summary and the doctor's **plan** showing how often a patient should be looked at in the ward.

How many times will the patient be looked at altogether in the first eight hours?

AFTER THE EMERGENCY

Some patients are discharged with a **prescription** for a medicine. They have to take the prescription to a pharmacy. The pharmacy counts out the correct number of tablets and writes instructions on the box on how to take the tablets.

Some patients are asked to come back to the hospital for a check up. These patients are given an 'out-patient' appointment to see the hospital doctor.

The hospital doctor may write a letter to the patient's family doctor (general practitioner or GP). The GP then knows if she has to follow up any of the results or if she needs to see the patient for a check up.

DATA BOX PATIENT'S SUMMARY

A patient's summary is shown below.

Complaint: head injury

History of complaint: fell off monkey bars in playground and bumped head

Examination: bruise on right side of forehead, otherwise normal

Diagnosis: minor head injury

Plan: observations every 15 minutes for the first hour, 30 minutes for the next two hours and once each hour for the next five hours.

A doctor checks a patient's records before agreeing they can go home.

CHALLENGE QUESTION

Approximately one in five of patients seen in accident and emergency are admitted to a ward, the rest are sent home (discharged).

a) What **percentage** of patients are discharged?
b) Write this number as a decimal.
c) Now write it as **fraction** in its simplest form.

(You will find a TIP to help you with this question on page 29)

TIPS FOR MATHS SUCCESS

PAGES 6–7

CHALLENGE QUESTION

Remember there are 1000 metres in 1 kilometre.

So 1500 metres = 1.5 kilometres
So 2800 metres = 2.8 kilometres and so on.

PAGES 8–9

EMERGENCY WORK

When writing dates, months are numbered, with January being the first month and December the twelth month. Dates are written using the day, month and year like this: 2-4-1991.
This means the 2nd of the 4th month (April) in the year 1991.

PAGES 10–11

CHALLENGE QUESTION

A pictogram should always have a key to tell you what one picture stands for. Here each circle means 4 people, so half a circle stands for 2 people.

PAGES 12–13

EMERGENCY WORK

To multiply by 4 you can double the number and double your answer:

25 x 4 Double 25 = 50
Double 50 = 100 So 25 x 4 = 100

CHALLENGE QUESTION

To divide by 4 you can halve the number and halve your answer

180 ÷4 Half 180 = 90
Half 90 = 45 So 180 ÷ 4 = 45

PAGES 14–15

EMERGENCY WORK

To find the difference between two times subtract (take away) the smaller number from the larger number. Be careful when you are subtracting minutes from an hour. Remember that there are 60 minutes in an hour.

PAGES 16–17

CHALLENGE QUESTIONS

When reading the graph to find the peak flow rate for a given height: go straight up from the height until you reach the line and then go across.

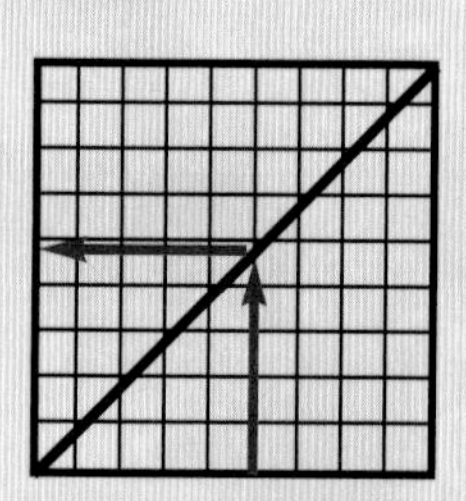

When reading the graph to find the height for a given peak flow rate: go straight across from the peak flow rate until you reach the line and then go down.

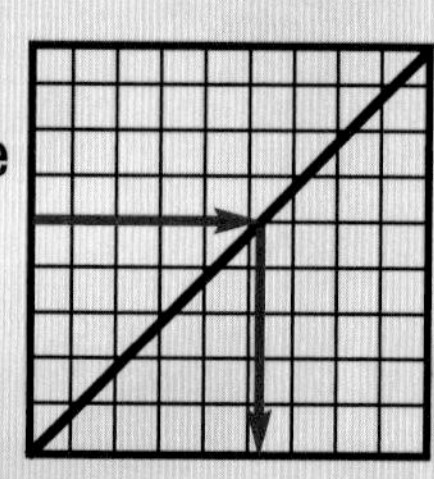

PAGES 18–19

Continuing sequences

If you are not sure how a number pattern (sequence) continues first find the difference between the numbers, like this
Then you'll know that the next number will be **4** more than 22 and so on.

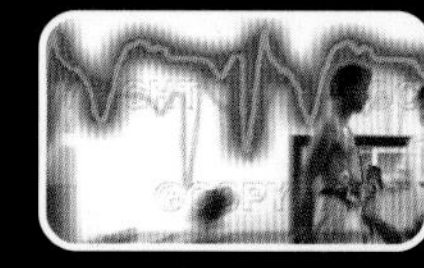

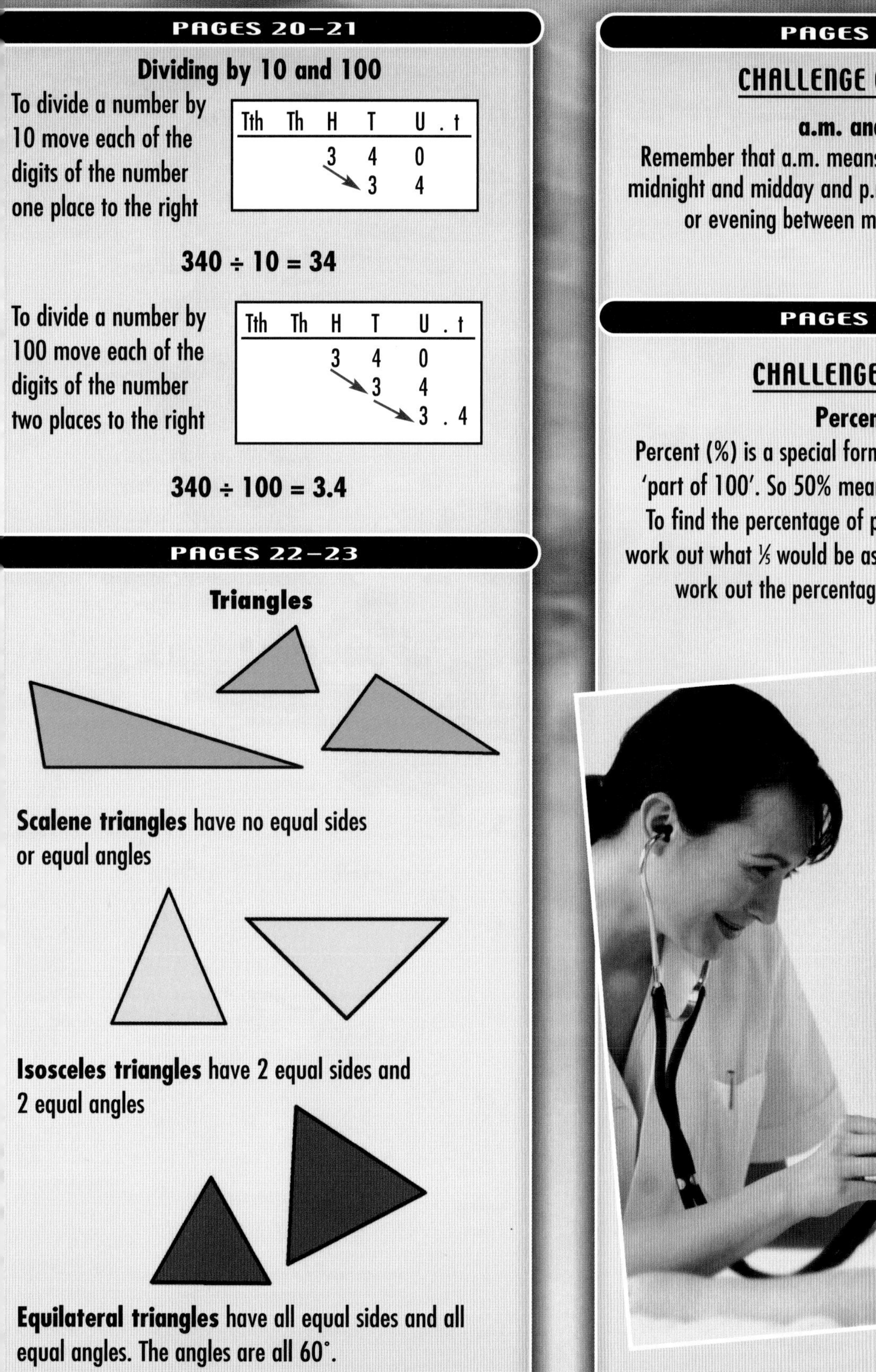

PAGES 20–21

Dividing by 10 and 100

To divide a number by 10 move each of the digits of the number one place to the right

Tth	Th	H	T	U . t
		3	4	0
			↘ 3	4

340 ÷ 10 = 34

To divide a number by 100 move each of the digits of the number two places to the right

Tth	Th	H	T	U . t
		3	4	0
			↘ 3	4
				↘ 3 . 4

340 ÷ 100 = 3.4

PAGES 22–23

Triangles

Scalene triangles have no equal sides or equal angles

Isosceles triangles have 2 equal sides and 2 equal angles

Equilateral triangles have all equal sides and all equal angles. The angles are all 60˚.

PAGES 24–25

CHALLENGE QUESTIONS

a.m. and p.m.

Remember that a.m. means in the morning between midnight and midday and p.m. means in the afternoon or evening between midday and midnight.

PAGES 26–27

CHALLENGE QUESTION

Percentages

Percent (%) is a special form of a fraction and it means 'part of 100'. So 50% means $\frac{50}{100}$ or in other words $\frac{1}{2}$. To find the percentage of people admitted to a ward, work out what $\frac{1}{5}$ would be as a percentage. Then you can work out the percentage of people sent home.

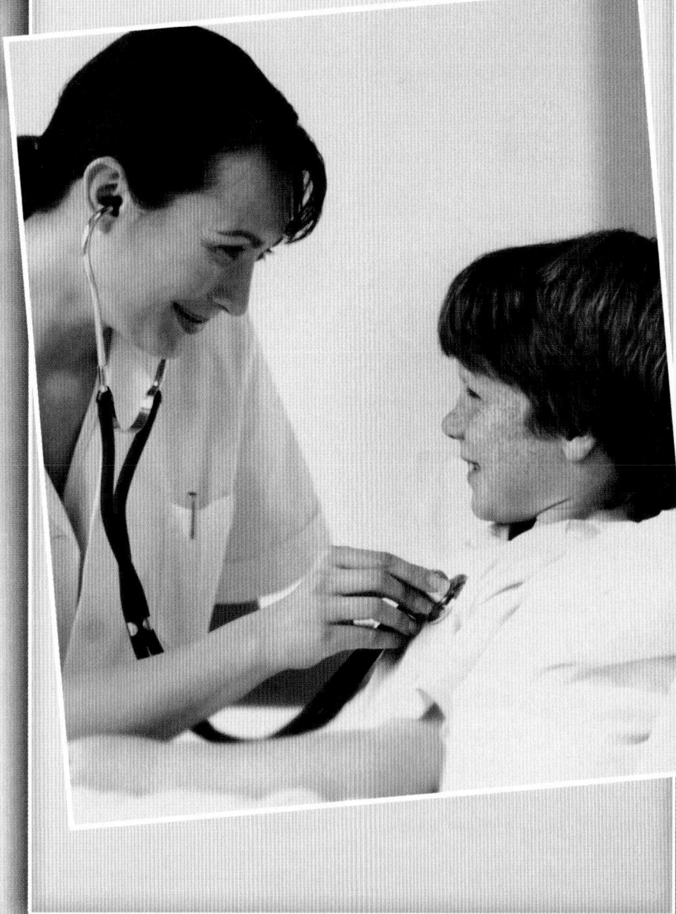

ANSWERS ANSWERS ANSWERS

PAGES 6–7

EMERGENCY WORK

After leaving the hospital, the quickest route is to take the first turn **left**, then turn **left** again. At the traffic lights turn **right**, then **left**, and then **right** again.

1) a) 3 b) 2
2) a) 4 b) 3
3) a) 3 b) 4

CHALLENGE QUESTIONS

1) 2200 m or 2.2 km
2) 1.375 miles

PAGES 8–9

EMERGENCY WORK

1) 211 months

2)

CHALLENGE QUESTION

Kamelia Court	**RED**
Jack Collins	**GREEN**
Daisy Barber	**BLUE**
Claire Smith	**ORANGE**
Deepa Gorasia	**YELLOW**
Arthur Miller	**YELLOW**

PAGES 10–11

EMERGENCY WORK

1) Suspected broken bones
2) Unconscious/semiconscious
3) a) 12 b) 16 c) 26 d) 10
4) 2 5) 10 6) 100

CHALLENGE QUESTION

About 90,000 patients

PAGES 12–13

EMERGENCY WORK

Jane	100	No problem
Luke	140	No problem
Dev	144	Pulse is too fast
Urvi	116	Pulse is too fast
Molly	124	No problem
Chelsea	76	Pulse is too slow

CHALLENGE QUESTION

a) 23 beats d) 18 beats
b) 19 beats e) 17 beats
c) 13 beats f) 22 beats

PAGES 14–15

EMERGENCY WORK

1) a) 39°C b) 37.5°C c) 37°C
2) 10:00
3) 08:45
4) 915 minutes, or 15 hours and 15 minutes

CHALLENGE QUESTION

1)

Blue whale	1.5°C cooler
Cow	1.5°C warmer
Dog	1°C warmer
Elephant	0.5°C cooler
Ostrich	2°C warmer
Owl	3°C warmer
Polar bear	same

2) 35.5°C, 36.5°C, 37°C, 38°C, 38.5°C, 39°C, 40°C

PAGES 16–17

EMERGENCY WORK

a) Ella 110 b) Robbie 170 c) Ben 140
d) Zack 40 e) Jess 140

CHALLENGE QUESTIONS

1) a) about 300 l/min b) about 400 l/min
c) about 180 l/min
2) a) about 120 cm b) about 150 cm
c) about 176 cm

PAGES 18–19

EMERGENCY WORK

a) 14, 16, 18
b) 30, 20, 10
c) 65, 70, 75
d) 21, 24, 27
e) 42, 47, 52
f) 5¾, 6¼, 6¾
g) 11, 14, 17
h) 9, 10.5, 12
i) 1.9, 2.1, 2.3

CHALLENGE QUESTION

a) red, yellow, blue
b) red, yellow, brown
c) blue, brown, yellow
d) blue, brown, red

PAGES 20–21

EMERGENCY WORK

1) a) 17 ml b) 20 ml c) 16 ml
2) a) 1.5 ml b) 1.3 ml c) 1.9ml
3) a) 1 ml b) 1.2 ml
4) a) 0.4 ml b) 0.7 ml

CHALLENGE QUESTION

find one quarter ⟷ divide by 4
find one tenth ⟷ divide by 10
find ⅕ ⟷ divide by 5
find 1/100 ⟷ divide by 100
find 1/50 ⟷ divide by 50
find one thousandth ⟷ divide by 1000
find one third ⟷ divide by 3
find ½ ⟷ divide by 2

PAGES 22–23

EMERGENCY WORK

1) a) isosceles d) isosceles
b) equilateral e) equilateral
c) scalene f) scalene
2) Triangles c and d have a right angle
3) a) 1 d) 1
b) 3 e) 3
c) 0 f) 0

CHALLENGE QUESTIONS

a) 6 days
b) 4½ days
c) 1½ days
d) 7½ days
e) 60 days
f) 75 days
g) 105 days

PAGES 24–25

EMERGENCY WORK

1) a) 24 b) 12 c) 20 d) 56
2) a) 6 hours apart c) 12 hours apart
b) 8 hours apart d) 6 hours apart

CHALLENGE QUESTIONS

1) a) 14:00, 20:00 and 02:00.
b) 22:15, 04:15 and 10:15
2) a) 23:00, 03:00, 07:00, 11:00, 15:00
b) 08:45, 12:45, 16:45, 20:45, 00:45

PAGES 26–27

EMERGENCY WORK

13 times
4 times in the first hour, twice in the second and third hours and once in each of the last five hours
4 + 2 + 2 + 1 + 1 + 1 + 1 + 1 = 13

CHALLENGE QUESTION

a) 80% b) 0.8 c) ⅘

ASTHMA An illness where the air passages you breathe through tighten.

ANTIHISTAMINE A drug that helps patients suffering from an allergic reaction.

DISCHARGED A patient that can go home.

ELEVATION Raising in the air.

HYPOTHERMIA A body temperature that is too low.

INHALER A device to help breathing that gives medicine in the form of a vapour.

INVESTIGATION Finding out what is wrong with a patient. It can be a test performed on the blood or urine, an x-ray or a scan of the patient.

LIGAMENT A band of tissue that connects two bones together.

OBSERVATION When a patient is regularly checked by a doctor.

PAEDIATRICS The branch of medicine that deals with the care of infants and children.

PARAMEDIC A person who is trained to give immediate emergency care.

PEAK FLOW METER A piece of equipment to measure how much breath is blown out in under a second.

PRESCRIBED The amount of a medicine given to a patient.

PULSE RATE The rate at which the heart pushes blood around the body.

RADIOGRAPHER A person who takes x-rays.

RESPIRATION Breathing.

RESUSCITATION To return to life.

STEROID A hormone that helps muscles and tissue to grow.

STETHOSCOPE A piece of equipment for listening to the heart and lungs.

STROKE A sudden loss of physical or mental ability, caused by a blood clot in the brain.

TRIAGE The system of deciding which patients should be treated first.

VITAL SIGN Measurement of pulse rate, blood pressure, respiratory rate or temperature.

MATHS GLOSSARY

DEGREES – the units used for measuring angle °, or temperature °C.

DIFFERENCE – the difference between two numbers can be found by subtracting (taking away) the smaller number from the larger number.

EQUILATERAL TRIANGLE – a triangle with all equal sides and all equal angles.

FRACTIONS – these are made when shapes or numbers are split into equal parts. For example, if a shape is cut into 6 equal parts each part is one sixth or ⅙.

l/min – an abbreviation standing for litres per minute.

ISOSCELES TRIANGLE – a triangle with 2 equal sides and 2 equal angles.

PERCENTAGE – a part out of 100.

PICTOGRAM – a chart where a picture is used to stand for several units.

SCALENE TRIANGLE – a triangle with no equal sides or equal angles.

SEQUENCE – a number pattern.

TEMPERATURE – how hot or cold something is. It is usually measured in degrees Celsius which are written using the symbols °C.

PICTURE CREDITS

Front cover: Ingram Publishing

Creatas: 1, 14-15, 22-23, 26-27

Shutterstock: 6-7 michael ledray, 20-21 Jaimie Duplass, 24 (inset) Jack Dagley Photography

StockDisc: 8-9, 10-11, 12-13, 18-19, 24-25

Science Photo Library: 16-17 Ian Hooton